_to_

from

on this date

when I'm on my knees

ANITA CORRINE DONIHUE

A DAYMAKER GREETING BOOK

"ALL WE CAN DO NOW IS PRAY." I SAID IT AGAIN! HOW SHORTSIGHTED CAN I BE ? (GREAT THINGS CAN HAPPEN WHILE WE'RE ON OUR KNEES.) THE FORCES OF HEAVEN ARE DISPERSED WHEN ONE PRAYS. THE VERY POWER THAT RAISED MY LORD JESUS FROM THE DEAD IS THERE FOR MY OWN NEEDS.

✞ THANK YOU THAT WHEN I BOW IN PRAYER, YOUR SON INTERCEDES ON MY BEHALF. IN HIS PURITY, HE BRINGS ALL MY REQUESTS BEFORE YOU. GIVE ME RIGHT MOTIVES AS I PRAY. GIVE ME FAITH TO RELEASE MY PRAYERS AND TO ENTRUST THEM TO YOUR KEEPING. ✞ REMIND ME OFTEN, LORD, THAT PRAYER CAN MOVE MOUNTAINS AND CHANGE HEARTS. ✞ FATHER, YOU KNOW ALL MY DESIRES. THANK YOU IN ADVANCE FOR ANSWERS THAT WILL COME ACCORDING TO YOUR WILL. ONLY YOU KNOW WHAT IS BEST. AMEN AND AMEN.

Give ear to my words, O LORD,

consider my meditation. . . .

My voice shalt thou hear

in the morning, O LORD;

in the morning will I direct my prayer

unto thee, and will look up.

PSALM 5:1, 3 KJV

Praise

Joyful, joyful, we adore Thee,

God of glory, Lord of love;

Hearts unfold like flowers before Thee,

Opening to the sun above.

Melt the clouds of sin and sadness,

Drive the dark of doubt away;

Giver of immortal gladness,

Fill us with the light of day.

HENRY VAN DYKE

✛

THANK YOU FOR YOUR WONDROUS WORKS

My thoughts often turn toward heaven, Lord. When earthly trials and worries surround me, I long to be with You. I feel homesick, as though I have some subconscious memory of having been in heaven before. Could I have been with You there before I was placed in my mother's womb? Someday I'll have the answers.

I don't feel a part of the evil in this world, and I'm certainly not attracted to what it has to offer. All the money I could earn, the treasure I can obtain, the land I may plan to buy, are nothing in light of my eternal home with You. Earthly things lose their value. They wear out, rust, fade, and are sometimes stolen. The eternal treasures I store in heaven with You can never be taken from me. So I'll invest my meager riches in You and Your work. I can't help but love You more than anything the world can give me.

Although my body will die, my soul grows closer to You with each passing day. All the trials and sufferings are minor and won't last. Thank You for the heavenly home I'll go to someday. There will be no sickness there, no pain, no tears. Only eternal life filled with joy and gladness awaits me. There I can be with You and praise You forever.

There is no fear in love.

But perfect love drives out fear,

because fear has to do with punishment.

The one who fears

is not made perfect in love.

We love because he first loved us.

1 John 4:18–19 NIV

Repentance

✠

I will greatly rejoice in the LORD, my soul shall be joyful in my God;

for he hath clothed me with the garments of salvation,

he hath covered me with the robe of righteousness,

as a bridegroom decketh himself with ornaments,

and as a bride adorneth herself with her jewels.

ISAIAH 61:10 KJV

GOSSIPING

I opened my mouth before I thought. Forgive me, Lord. How could I have talked so behind someone's back? I can never retrieve careless words. Give me strength to ask for forgiveness, to try to make things right. Go before me, dear Lord, and help me make amends.

I am beginning to realize gossip cuts to the core. Wise words soothe and heal. Teach me, Lord, to use words of wisdom, and in the future let me remember the hard lesson from this experience. Guard my tongue and seal my lips. The Bible shows me that careless words can break bones.

May I not get caught in the snares of others who are gossiping. Help me to build up life's cornerstones in people rather than chiseling and breaking them down.

Fill my thoughts with things that are good and right. Let everything I do and say be pleasing to You. Now, I focus my eyes on You, dear Lord. I take refuge in Your strength and comfort in Your wisdom.

✝

Peacemakers who sow in peace raise a harvest of righteousness.

JAMES 3:18 NIV

The Argument

Lord, I did it again. I fell into another argument and spoke unkindly. Why was I so thoughtless? My heart feels heavy; I find myself replaying the disagreement all day. Can I be wrong although I know I'm "right"? Is my attitude pure, unconditional love?

Calm my emotions and help us to show respect, to listen and not argue.

When I must disagree, help me express my feelings with love, doing my best to keep this person's dignity intact. Show me how to separate the essential from the trivial and to know where I should give in. In spite of our differences, I must remain accepting of the one I love.

Has it been seventy times seven that I have forgiven? Help me show gentleness and forgiveness as You do. Let me be willing not to hold a grudge. Teach me to go beyond myself with thoughtfulness and kindness during this time, remembering that perfect love casts out fear.

Surround me and my loved one with Your presence and keep us nestled in Your pure, sweet love.

"Forgive and you will be forgiven."

LUKE 6:37 NIV

forgiveness

✠

GOD MADE A WAY

No matter how hard she tried, Susan couldn't forgive her daughter Alyssa and her friends for what they had done during their rebellious teenage years. Now an adult, something was keeping Alyssa from living a victorious Christian life. Susan prayed for her often but couldn't identify the problem.

The Lord spoke to Susan's heart. He showed her that until she could forgive, she too was in sin. He helped her realize the hurt and anger she felt were linked together and that she had to let go of both in order to truly forgive. Susan asked God to help her forgive and let go of the painful memories.

The next time Alyssa came to visit, Susan's heart was free from fear, hurt, and bitterness. She and Alyssa took a long walk on a hiking trail shortly before the daughter was to return to her own home. As they walked and visited, Alyssa noticed something different about her mother and asked what it was. The mother told Alyssa how God had helped her change. She assured her daughter of the pride and of the unconditional love she felt for Alyssa. A bond of joy and freedom they hadn't experienced for years returned to mother and daughter. No excuses for shortcomings were offered by either—just "sorries" and forgiveness.

Soon after, Alyssa's love for the Lord matured. Susan felt thankful she was finally able to forgive, love, and step out of God's way, so He could work.

Jesus! what a friend for sinners!

Jesus! lover of my soul;

Friends may fail me

foes assail me,

He, my Savior, makes me whole.

J. WILBUR CHAPMAN

May the words of my mouth

and the meditation of my heart

be pleasing in your sight,

O LORD, my Rock and my Redeemer.

PSALM 19:14 NIV

Dedication

✠

OUT OF CONTROL

One of the most difficult things about dedicating our all to God is to relinquish control. We don't know what He has in store for us. Fearful it may be too difficult or uncomfortable, we often won't let go.

We must remember that God knows our future; He has our concerns and best interests at heart. Along the way we may not understand the reasons for His direction. As we continue walking by faith in the paths He blazes, we'll learn His answers.

Take each step; obey, and fear not. One day, one moment at a time is all He asks. When troubles come, look to Him; plant your feet on His path, and dig in your toes. Don't waver! He'll show the best way. He has already walked the path.

✠

BALANCING THE BUDGET

Dear Father, how can I pay these bills? Sometimes I don't even know where food money will come from. I'm working as hard as possible, but on paper I can't meet the budget.

I give it to You, dear Lord. I place myself and these bills in Your hands and ask for Your direction. Show me how I can help others even while I hurt financially. Help me share a portion of my earnings with You for Your glory. Remind me to give You first place in my pocket book!

Teach me to be prudent in my spending, wise in my financial decisions, and responsible in attempting to pay my obligations.

Enable me to trust You to provide for my needs so I won't worry about food or drink, money or clothes. You already know my needs. I thank You for providing. Let me not be anxious about tomorrow. I know You will take care of that, too. I will take each day as it comes and commit it to You.

I will trust You, Lord, and not lean on my own understanding of these situations. With all my heart, I will recognize Your will to direct my paths.

Search me, O God, and know

my heart; test me and know my

anxious thoughts. See if there is

any offensive way in me, and

lead me in the way everlasting.

PSALM 139:23–24 NIV

✠

I Dedicate My Heart to You

Father, I give You my heart, my soul, my life. I dedicate my whole being to You. I give You my failures and my successes, my fears and my aspirations. Search my heart. Let my thoughts and motives be pure. You know me through and through. Remove the unclean ways in me that I might be pleasing to You.

Fill me with Your spirit, I pray: enable me to do the tasks set before me. Lead me into Your everlasting way.

Wherever I go, whatever the challenge, I pray that You will be there, guiding me completely. From my rising in the morn to my resting at night, O Lord, be near, surrounding me continually with Your love.

I look forward with joyful anticipation to what You have planned for me. Thank You for becoming Lord of my life.

The grass withereth,

the flower fadeth:

but the word of our God

shall stand for ever.

Grieving

✛

My Loved One Is Gone

Dear Lord, I miss my loved one so. There's a huge gap in my life. Will it ever be filled? In all this, I am grateful for friends and family who show they care. Comfort and help me find my way through all of this. Let me recall and cherish the good times, to let the bad memories go.

How will I bear my loss? I long for the company of one who was so full of life like the roses outside my window. As my roses will fade from winter's chill, so, too, have I seen my loved one fade. I gaze at my lovely garden with its splendid array of color. I'm reminded that my dear one who loved You will blossom in full glory for You in heaven.

I take comfort in Your presence and know you will always abide with me.

Lord, I can hardly stand all the hurts and sin in this world as I'm forced to brush shoulders with it daily. Thank You for loving me in my weakest moments. Loved ones and friends fall away from you, marriages dissolve. Little children suffer from abuse, illness, and neglect. Lord, take me home. I'm tired of being here. I feel ashamed to pray this way. But, oh, the pain.

"Not my will, but Thine be done." If you need to keep me here, so be it, dear Lord, although I long to be with You. As long as You have a purpose for me, I will serve You with all my heart. Grant me strength, I pray. And, Father, when You're finished with me here, I'm ready to come home to You.

TAKE ME HOME

What is this tugging at my heart?
'Tis like a homing dove.
How can I long for a place unseen
And feel His endless love?

Homesick and worn, I strive each day,
A broken soul to love.
But my broken heart aches to join
My Savior up above.

How long must I fight the battles
On tearstained fields for Thee?
"Until your task is finished here,"
He firmly says to me.

"I've covered your scars with my blood,
I've washed your hands and feet,
I've taken the sins of your soul
To the mercy seat."

What love I feel in His voice,
His hands outstretched to me.
I'll serve until that moment,
His loving face I see.

But they that wait upon the LORD

shall renew their strength;

they shall mount up with wings as eagles;

they shall run, and not be weary;

...they shall walk, and not faint.

ISAIAH 40:31 KJV

Healing

MY CHILD IS NOT WHOLE

Dear Lord, help my child who isn't whole. Why does my little one have to be this way? Why does such a precious child have these deficiencies? Sometimes I blame myself. If I had done this or that, would it have made a difference? My heart aches, longing for things to be better. I wish I could understand.

I love my child so much. Even though this dear one is disabled, to me I have the most wonderful little one in the world. I thank You for giving me such a sweet gift. Could my child be an angel in disguise?

Grant me patience daily, yet give me determination and consistency. Give me wisdom as I expect my child to do the best that abilities provide, yet let me be realistic in my expectations. Remind me to praise and accent the little accomplishments; help me build self-esteem. Let me cherish each day for the good times. Grant me strength when I am weak and weary; a calm spirit when I am frustrated.

Use this child, I pray, to be a blessing for You and those nearby. Let me learn from my experiences, and let me be of help to others with children who also are not whole.

Thank You, Lord, for giving me my child. Remind me that in Your eyes this little one is whole.

✛

BURNED OUT

Lord, I let myself get caught up in doing too many things. I'm burned out, so burned out I don't want to go anywhere or do anything. Bitterness and resentment are creeping in. Forgive me, Lord, and heal me. During this time of weakness, let me wait on You. Renew my strength, Lord, that I too can mount like the eagle. Please clip my wings just a little to keep me near You, to learn my limitations.

Let me put Your will first in my life, not the will of others. Give me the strength to say, "No thank you," in a loving, but firm way. Help me not to feel guilty. Perhaps I'm cheating others from the chance to serve.

Grant me wisdom in setting the right priorities: You first, my family second, and others next. Somewhere in there show me how to take time for me.

You are the Holy One of my life. I wonder, as You run an entire universe, how can You be concerned with the likes of me? I praise You, O Lord, that You consider me a treasure and that You love me with Your unconditional and everlasting love.

Give me time to mend. In Your own time, send me forth to work again for You. But for now, help me to lie back and absorb Your healing strength.

But the LORD is my defence;

and my God is the rock of my refuge.

Trials

✠

SINGING IN THE STORMS

The storms of life surround me, but I will not be tossed to and fro. I am anchored in Your steadfast love. A song of praise wells up from my heart. I will sing praise and glory to Your name while You carry me through this, another storm. You alone know the answers and the outcome. I take comfort in Your mighty presence.

I turn into the wind, unafraid, ready to face each day head-on, flanked with Your power and wisdom. In the peak of the storm, when I feel I can hold on no longer, I will call on Your name for peace. I will trust in You and will not feel afraid, as I nestle into Your protecting hands.

How is it that You have such mighty power, that the tempests in my life cease their crashing winds at Your command? How is it that You can calm my raging seas of circumstances and emotions and bring my life into Your control with Your powerful, yet hushed voice?

Even now, I hear Your whisper, "Peace, be still. Know I am your God." When storms subside, my song of praise for You will echo throughout the ages from generation to generation, telling of Your mighty works and deeds.

PICKING UP THE PIECES

Father, I am broken. I am running on empty. I have nothing to offer. Take the pieces of my
life; pick them up, I pray, and rearrange them. I know You are the Master Craftsman and
know my very being. Thank You for the miracles You create from my shattered life.
Thank You for how You are making me into a beautiful new vessel to be used for You.
In Jesus' name, I pray.

From birth, Sandra had been abused. No one knew about the physical and emotional hurt—it was almost unbearable. God helped her. He provided friends who led Sandra to know Christ as her Savior.

After high school, Sandra moved away but couldn't be free from hurt and anger. God helped her again.

One Sunday she went to a nearby church. The people showed her the love she so desperately needed. Sandra's new pastor and his wife spent hours of prayer and Bible study with Sandra, and she learned to give the hurts and bitterness to God. Yet the pain returned.

Sandra went with friends to a women's retreat. Between speakers she slipped away to a prayer chapel and met with the Lord again. She told Him she couldn't continue with the hurt and grief any longer. It was there, God reminded Sandra He was her Father; that He loved the fragile little girl within her. Sandra felt as if He wrapped His arms around her and took all her burdens on His shoulders.

Sandra accepted God's comfort and healing. She found peace. When pain and bad memories returned, she gave them back to the Lord, her Healer and heavenly Father.

Thou art my hiding place;

thou shalt preserve me from trouble;

thou shalt compass me about

with songs of deliverance.

PSALM 32:7 KJV

Deliverance

✠

"Never will I leave you; never will I forsake you."
"The Lord is my helper; I will not be afraid."

HEBREWS 13:5–6 NIV

I DON'T LIKE MY JOB

Dear Father, I pray You will help me with my job. Things aren't going right. I dread going to work and I need Your direction. On days I feel I'm doing more than my share, may my attitude be right. Give me wisdom, I pray. When I do menial tasks, help me remember when Your Son, though King of Kings, came down from heaven and often acted as a servant. Let me not be too proud to serve.

Help me to be honest in estimating my own abilities, to not put myself down or become a braggart. Teach me to appreciate a job well done, to feel an inner sense of accomplishment. I lean on You, not only on my skills. I know I can earn my pay and make a living; or I can give of myself and make a life.

Go before me when there is friction or backbiting. Let my motives be pure and uplifting, relying on Your help, so Your light can shine through.

"Hey!" shouted Dad. "I can see clearly through this camera. It's like a filter." I trusted Dad as he calmly directed me. We reached a traffic jam in a nearby tunnel. I tried to appear calm for Dad's sake, but I was almost in tears.

Please, Lord, I prayed. *Move the storm and help us find our way.* The song, "Wonderful Grace of Jesus" whirred through my mind like a revolving tape. We approached the tunnel's opening and the sheet of rain. I nosed the car out. At the same time, a gust of wind moved the storm to our right like the parting of the Red Sea. Before long we made it to our destination.

At times I find myself struggling and losing my way. Then I remember Montreal. God doesn't always move or end the storms, but He calms my spirit, and He gives me a song for courage. As I obey Him and read His Word, He guides me along life's freeways.

It's easy in our fast-paced world to let life control our schedules. Before long, we find our days filled with jumble, wasted time, an overabundance of television, senseless actions, going nowhere. Like spinning wheels on a slippery freeway, we lose our spiritual footing, become irritable and frustrated. Our songs of praise and worship (when we listen to them) ring in our ears like fast-forward recordings. No concept. No application. No direction.

Pull off life's fast lane for awhile—turn to God for direction and strength. Tune in to His voice and marvel as He prepares the way. As we seek His direction, miraculously He makes more time in our day. At night, we can look back and be satisfied within His will.

"But as for me and my household,

we will serve the LORD."

JOSHUA 24:15 NIV

✠

Thank You for This Special Day

Lord, I collapse onto our couch, kick my shoes off, and think of today's blessings. Family and friends bustled around. Children chattered with youthful excitement. Steaming irresistible foods simmered in the kitchen. Men exchanged stories and (thank You, Lord) helped with the little ones. It seems a whooshing dream; the day went so fast.

I reflect briefly on the struggles we've all had, the mountains we've fearfully conquered with Your help. Still we're together, loving and sharing. It was worth listening to each other and finding Your will through the years. I'm tired, but I loved it all. At nightfall, little arms wrapped around my neck with an "I love you, Nana." Strong embraces from sons so dear and tender hugs from loving daughters filled my heart with joy. When did I earn such love and honor? I don't know, but I thank You for it, Lord. I treasure the look of pleasure and pride, the squeeze of a hand from my own dear parents.

Now the silence is here, ringing its tranquil melody. I lean over and nuzzle my head on my husband's shoulder. His look is one of fulfillment and approval. Love softly drifts between us.

I thank You, Lord, for for the love of family and friends.

As special days end in all their wild flurry, I'm often reminded of the true value in it all: not food, fancies, and elaborations, but my dearest friends and loved ones.

✣

From Calamity to Calm

Father, this day has too much responsibility for me. My head spins with frustration. My life is full of calamity. Help me to gain Your perspective. When my footing begins to slip, let me cling to You, my Fortress. Instill Your direction in my cluttered mind. When I am weak, lend me Your quiet, confident strength; when impatient, grant me Your patience. If I fail, help me not to keep punishing myself, but to leave it in Your hands and go on.

Teach me to eliminate those things that are unnecessary and to concentrate on the essentials. Help me slow down enough to take time for myself and You.

Keep my thoughts accurate, my hands sure, and my feet swift in doing Your will. Remind me of my limitations, Lord. Keep my step close behind—not in front of—You and protect me with Your strong hands.

At the day's end, I will lie down and reflect on all I have learned. I will recall how much You have helped me. I will praise You with great joy as I drift off to sleep, nestled in the protection of Your mighty wings.

I will instruct you and teach you in the way you should go;
I will counsel you and watch over you.

PSALM 32:8 NIV

43

A friend loveth at all times.

Love

☩

Love? I will tell you what it is to love!
It is to build with human hearts a shrine,
Where hope sits brooding like a beauteous dove,
Where time seems young, and life a thing divine.

CHARLES SWAIN

THANK YOU FOR MY FRIEND

She was there, again, right when I needed a listening ear and a shoulder to lean on. Thank You for my friend, Lord. She is so special to me. Whenever we can't see each other, there are little thought waves going back and forth between us and little "arrow prayers" going up for one another during the day.

Thank You for my friend when she brings over a tray of cookies and I pour the tea. Amidst the work, our world stops while we take a little time for each other's company.

Help me never to take my friend for granted but to treat her with thoughtfulness. Help me to recognize when she wants my company and when she needs time alone.

I know we will remain close for years to come. For every year we have, I am thankful.

✠

These three remain: faith, hope and love.
But the greatest of these is love.

1 CORINTHIANS 13:13 NIV

THANK YOU FOR THE MAN I LOVE

He gazes at me from across the packed room. We're at just another meeting, but I dressed to look my best. Do I see the same twinkle in his eyes I saw when we first met? Do I see the same look he wore on our wedding day? Am I so blessed that he still gazes at me with the same love and pride? Thank You, Lord, for that look. Thank You for today and for him.

Help me show to him the same love and thoughtfulness as when we first married. In our hurried schedules, let us look for time to spend with each other. Sometimes I love even sharing a second glass of iced tea on the patio at sundown.

I think of changes we've faced. We have fallen in love with each other over and over again, even in the midst of change.

Teach us to keep respecting one another's feelings. Teach us to put each other first, after You.

And, Lord, help me keep myself in a way that he will always look across the room with love and pride.

O LORD God of hosts,

who is a strong LORD like unto thee?

or to thy faithfulness round about thee?

PSALM 89:8 KJV

faithfulness

✠

Our Newborn Baby

Tiny fingers wrapped around mine, Daddy's proud gaze; a little darling rests securely in my arms. Already my heart overflows with love. I talked to and prayed for this sweet one even before giving birth. What does our baby's future hold? Prepare the way that our child may grow up to love and serve You. Grant my husband and I wisdom in raising such a precious gift.

Today, O Lord, I dedicate our baby as a love offering to You. Like Hannah in days of old, I thank You for giving our little one to us. Here and now, I present our child at Your altar to be raised for Your service.

Let Your angels encamp around and about, and protect from evil and harm. Help us teach Your ways by truth and example. When we err, I pray, dear Lord, that You will help meet the needs and forgive us. Place Christians in life's pathway. I pray that You will create a special hunger in this little heart to know, love, and serve You completely.

Help me remember our child is lent to us for a little while and that You are the Lender. Let me not take our dear one back from You or pursue my own ways outside Your will.

I will bless Your name, O Lord, thanking You for this wonderful infant gift. I praise Your name in my thoughts, motives, and actions forever.

✝

THE REBELLIOUS CHILD

Father, help my rebelling child. I'm overwhelmed with worry. Have I caused this child, once little and carefree, to go astray? Will my dear one's mistakes cause a lifetime of suffering? Is it all or partly my fault?

Forgive me, O Lord, for the wrongs I have caused. Let me humble myself and ask this loved one's forgiveness. Let me offer no excuses. Cleanse my heart from bitterness and give me a pure, unconditional love. Grant me wisdom. Teach me when to be lenient, when to be firm. Help me have motives that are pure, honest, and aboveboard. Remind me not to try fixing things.

Place Your angels about my child. Protect from sin, and lead my child to Your perfect will. Soften our hearts. Give us both a hunger to love and serve You.

Now, dear Lord, I release control of my beloved child to You. I will trust You in every situation and timing. Even when I don't understand why, still will I trust and praise You. Through these troublesome times I know You are helping and keeping my dear one in Your care.

Thank You for victories to come. Thank You for hearing my prayers. Thank You that You can go places with my child that I can't. As the answers to prayer come, may I write them down and remember them. Praise You, O God, for Your mighty works. In You I put my total trust.

However, I consider my life

worth nothing to me,

if only I may finish the race and

complete the task

the Lord Jesus has given me—

the task of testifying to

the gospel of God's grace.

ACTS 20:24 NIV

Challenge

"Blessed is the man who trusts in the LORD,
whose confidence is in him.
He will be like a tree planted by the water
that sends out its roots by the stream."

JEREMIAH 17:7-8 NIV

My husband Bob and I have five, now fine grown sons. Reflecting on their teen years, we recall happy memories, but also some frightening moments.

During the rebellious, emotional times we discovered valuable lessons. First, we learned to hold a steady, consistent course so our kids could have something stable to look toward. If we strayed in the slightest, it magnified in our children. They challenged everything we said and did.

As our children attempted to find their own way, they tested us for purity and validity. No amount of speeches or attempts to set them straight worked. Communication, listening, and love helped most. We also soon discovered our example meant much more than mere words.

Another lesson learned was to maintain a close fellowship with our Lord. He was our Guide, our Counselor, Friend, and source of strength. And so, we were able to offer and offer again each child to God. He went with them where we couldn't and spoke to each one when our words didn't reach them.

Now we praise God for His miracles and answered prayers and for our beloved family. We still hold those six-foot sons, our precious daughters by marriage, and now our grandchildren up to God and leave them in His care .

Hear the Prayer We Offer

Father, hear the prayer we offer;
Not for ease that prayer shall be,
But for strength that we may ever
Live our lives courageously.

Not forever in green pastures
Do we ask our way to be,
But the steep and rugged pathway
May we tread rejoicingly.

Not forever by still waters
Would we idly quiet stay,
But would smite the living fountains
From the rocks along the way.

Be our strength in hours of weakness;
In our wanderings be our guide;
Through endeavor, failure, danger,
Father, be Thou at our side. Amen.

LOVE M. WILLIS

If you enjoyed this book, look for the best-selling

When I'm on My Knees

wherever books are sold.

© 2002 by Barbour Publishing, Inc.
ISBN 1-58660-706-5

Cover images ©Yuen Lee/Photonica
Book design by Kevin Keller| designconcepts

All Scripture quotations, unless otherwise noted,
are taken from the King James Version of the Bible.

Scripture quotations marked NIV are taken from the HOLY BIBLE,
NEW INTERNATIONAL VERSION®. NIV®. Copyright © 1973, 1978, 1984 by International Bible
Society. Used by permission of Zondervan Publishing House. All rights reserved.

Published by Barbour Books, an imprint of Barbour Publishing, Inc.,
P.O. Box 719, Uhrichsville, Ohio 44683. www.barbourbooks.com

Member of the
Evangelical Christian
Publishers Association

Printed in China.
5 4 3 2 1